Miracles of Jesus

by
Christopher P. N. Maselli

Carson-Dellosa Publishing Company, Inc.
Greensboro, North Carolina

It is the mission of Carson-Dellosa to create the highest-quality Scripture-based children's products that teach the Word of God, share His love and goodness, assist in faith development, and glorify His Son, Jesus Christ.

". . . teach me your ways so I may know you. . . ."
Exodus 33:13

Credits

Editors.................. Kathie Szitas, Carol Layton
Inside Illustrations......... Christian Elden
Cover Design .... Van Harris
Cover Illustration.......... Marci McAdam

Scripture taken from the HOLY BIBLE, New International Reader's Version®. Copyright © 1973, 1978, 1984 by International Bible Society. Used by permission of Zondervan Publishing House. All rights reserved.

© 2008, Carson-Dellosa Publishing Company, Inc., Greensboro, North Carolina 27425. The purchase of this material entitles the buyer to reproduce activities and worksheets for home or classroom use only–not for commercial resale. Reproduction of these materials for an entire school or district is prohibited. No part of this book may be reproduced (except as noted above), stored in a retrieval system, or transmitted in any form or by any means (mechanically, electronically, recording, etc.) without the prior written consent of Carson-Dellosa Publishing Co., Inc.

Printed in the USA • All rights reserved.   ISBN: 978-1-60022-519-2

Table of Contents

Water into Wine 4

The Woman at the Well 5

Healed With a Word 6

So Many Fish 7

Healing Peter's Mother-in-Law 8

Going through the Roof 9

Healing at the Pool 10

Authority to Heal 11

Jesus Calms the Storm 12

Standing Out in a Crowd 13

Jairus's Daughter 14

Do you Believe? 15

A Feast for 5,000 16

Jesus Walks on Water 17

Miracles Galore 18

Sight to the Blind 19

Mustard Seed–Sized Faith 20

Tax Time 21

10 Healed, 1 Thankful 22

Blind from Birth 23

Lazarus Raised from the Dead 24

Healed on the Sabbath 25

Jesus Is Alive! 26

Whole-Group Activities 27

Answer Key 31

Name _____

Water into Wine

Read John 2:1–11. Jesus' first public miracle was turning water into wine. When He did this, people realized God's power was with Him. Jesus' disciples put their faith in Him. Jesus still performs miracles every day. People's lives change for the better, and their lives are proof that God's power still works. **Look for His miracles every day!**

Find and circle two matching water jugs in the picture below. Color the rest of the picture.

That was the first of Jesus' miraculous signs. He did it at Cana in Galilee.
Jesus showed his glory by doing it. And his disciples put their faith in him. John 2:11

The Woman at the Well

Read John 4:4–26 and 39–42. One day, Jesus met a woman who was getting water from a well. She didn't know Jesus and was surprised that He would even talk to her. He told her things only God would know. She told her friends what happened, and they went to meet Jesus, too. **When you tell others what Jesus has done for you, it will help them get to know Him themselves.**

Number the pictures 1-4 to put the story in the correct order. Color the pictures.

"We no longer believe just because of what you said. We have now heard for ourselves. We know that this man really is the Savior of the world." John 4:42

Name _____

Healed With a Word

Read John 4:46–54. A man asked Jesus to come to his home and heal his son who was close to death. Jesus did not go. Instead, He told the man, "Your son will live." The man believed Jesus. When he got home, his son was perfectly well! When the man asked when his son had recovered, he was told the time. It was the exact moment Jesus had said, "Your son will live." **You can take Jesus at His Word. What He says is always true. You can trust Him to do what He says He will do.**

Connect the dots 0–33. Color the picture.

Jesus replied, "You may go. Your son will live."
The man believed what Jesus said, and so he left. John 4:50

Name _____

So Many Fish

Read Luke 5:1–11. After fishing all night, Simon Peter had caught nothing. Jesus told him to try again. When he did, so many fish jumped into Simon Peter's net, it started to break! Because Simon Peter obeyed Jesus, a miracle happened. **If you obey Jesus, you'll be ready to see miracles, too.**

Find and circle the two matching fish. Color the picture.

Simon answered, "Master, we've worked hard all night and haven't caught anything. But because you say so, I will let down the nets." Luke 5:5

Healing Peter's Mother-in-Law

Read Luke 4:38–39. Jesus went to His disciple Peter's house. Peter's mother-in-law was in bed with a high fever. The disciples asked Jesus to help her. Jesus touched Peter's mother-in-law, and at once, the fever went away. **Jesus cares about your family, too. Always remember to pray for each member of your family. Your prayers make a difference!**

What did the disciples do to help Peter's mother-in-law? Use the code to fill in the answer.

† = A   ✿ = E   ☺ = O   ❈ = U

TH __ Y __ SK __ D J __ S __ S
    ✿   †   ✿   ✿   ❈

T __ H __ LP H __ R.
  ☺   ✿   ✿

He bent over her and commanded the fever to leave, and it left her. She got up at once and began to serve them. Luke 4:39

Going through the Roof

Read Mark 2:1–12. Four men brought their paralyzed friend to Jesus for healing. The house where Jesus was preaching was so crowded, they couldn't get to Him. So, they climbed onto the roof and cut out a hole to lower their friend through! When Jesus saw their faith, He spoke to the paralyzed man. The man immediately got up, took his mat, and walked out the door. **Don't ever let anyone stop you from going to Jesus for help. He is waiting for you.**

Find and circle the objects hidden in the picture. Color the picture.

Jesus saw their faith. So he said to the man, "Son, your sins are forgiven." Mark 2:5

Healing at the Pool

Read John 5:1–15. Jesus found a man by a pool who had been ill for 38 years. He had been at the pool day after day, trying to get to the water to be healed, because other people had been healed that way. But Jesus healed him immediately. **When you need help, don't try all of the things other people do first and** *then* **go to Jesus. Go to Jesus first. You are sure to find the exact answer you need.**

How can you go to Jesus? To find out, start at the letter **P** and go around the circle of this pool, crossing out every other letter. Write the answer on the lines below.

___ ___ ___

___ ___

___ ___ ___ ___ ___

"Sir," the disabled man replied, "I have no one to help me into the pool when an angel stirs the water up. I try to get in, but someone else always goes down ahead of me." John 5:7

Authority to Heal

Read Matthew 8:5–13. A Roman officer approached Jesus about his servant who needed healing. Jesus said he would go to the officer's house and heal the servant. But the officer told Jesus that He didn't need to do that. The officer knew how authority worked because he was a boss. He knew that when he said something, his servants obeyed him. In the same way, he knew Jesus was boss over sickness, and if Jesus said the word, sickness had to obey. Jesus said the word, and the officer's servant was healed! **If sickness, or anything else, tries to boss you around, don't put up with it! Instead, go to Jesus. He has authority over it all!**

Draw a line through the maze to help the Roman officer get to his servant.

Then Jesus said to the Roman commander,
"Go! It will be done just as you believed it would." Matthew 8:13

Name _____

Jesus Calms the Storm

Read Luke 8:22–25. Jesus and His disciples were caught in a dangerous storm. The disciples were scared and asked Jesus for help. Jesus stood and told the storm to stop. Immediately, the rain and wind calmed. **When things get rough in your life, you can ask Jesus for help, too. He's able to calm any storm.**

Circle the letters to the word **MIRACLE** hidden in the picture. Color the picture.

They were amazed and full of fear. They asked one another,
"Who is this? He commands even the winds and the waves, and they obey him." Luke 8:25

Name _____

Standing Out in a Crowd

Read Mark 5:24–34. One day, Jesus and his disciples were walking through a crowd. A woman who had a bleeding sickness for 12 years touched the edge of Jesus' clothing. Immediately, she was healed. Jesus stopped and asked who had touched Him. His disciples didn't understand why Jesus would ask that because so many people were touching Him. But Jesus knew the woman had reached out to Him with faith and was healed. **There may be billions of people on the earth, but Jesus knows exactly where you are and what you need. To Him, you always stand out in a crowd.**

Connect the dots 0–25. Color the picture.

Then she heard about Jesus. She came up behind him in the crowd and touched his clothes. She thought, "I just need to touch his clothes. Then I will be healed." Mark 5:27–28

Name _____

Jairus's Daughter

Read Luke 8:40–42 and 49–56. A man named Jairus told Jesus that his 12-year-old daughter was dying. Jesus was on the way to her when someone from Jairus' house came and said it was too late–Jairus's daughter was dead. Jesus told Jairus not to be afraid, but to believe. Jesus went straight to Jairus's house and told the girl to get up. At once, she did! **God is never late. He knows just when you need Him, and He knows just what to do.**

Find and circle the words in the word-search puzzle. The words can be found horizontally and vertically. Write the remaining letters in order from left to right on the lines below to find out what Jesus tells all of us to do.

RULER	GIRL	JAIRUS	SYNAGOGUE	ASLEEP
DYING	TWELVE	LIVE	SPIRIT	HEALED
LUKE	MIRACLE	JESUS		

```
R U L E R D D Y I N G T
O N L U K E O G I R L W
T M I R A C L E B E A E
J A I R U S L I V E F L
E R S Y N A G O G U E V
S A S P I R I T I D J E
U A S L E E P U S T B E
S L I E H E A L E D V E
```

___ ___ ___ ___ ___ ___ ___ ___ ___ ___ ___ .

___ ___ ___ ___ ___ ___ ___ ___ ___ ___ ___ .

Hearing this, Jesus said to Jairus, "Don't be afraid. Just believe. She will be healed." Luke 8:50

Name _____

Do You Believe?

Read Matthew 9:27–30. Two blind men followed Jesus and asked Him to heal their eyes. Jesus had one question for them: "Do you believe that I am able to do this?" They both said they did. Then, He touched their eyes, and they could see! **If you need healing or help from God, ask yourself this question: "Do you believe He is able to do it?"** God loves to see your faith.

What does Hebrews 11 say faith does? Use this code to find out. Write the answer on the lines below. Color the picture.

| 1 = T | 2 = S | 3 = P | 4 = O | 5 = L | 6 = I |
| 7 = H | 8 = G | 9 = F | 10 = E | 11 = D | 12 = A |

__ __ __ __ __
9 12 6 1 7

__ __ __ __ __ __ __   __ __ __
3 5 10 12 2 10 2   8 4 11

Then he touched their eyes. He said, "It will happen to you just as you believed." They could now see again. Matthew 9:29–30

A Feast for 5,000

Read Matthew 14:12–21. One day, more than 5,000 people came to listen to Jesus teach. Hours passed, and Jesus knew that they were hungry. He asked His disciples what they had to feed the people. The disciples told Jesus all that they had were five loaves of bread and two fish. Jesus took what they had, blessed it, and told the disciples to feed it to the crowd. Miraculously, not only was there enough food for everyone, but there were also 12 baskets of leftovers! **When you give what you have to Jesus, He will always make sure that you have more than enough.**

Connect the dots 0–39. Color the picture.

All of them ate and were satisfied. The disciples picked up 12 baskets of leftover pieces. The number of men who ate was about 5,000. Women and children also ate. Matthew 14:20–21

Name _____

Jesus Walks on Water

Read Matthew 14:22–33. The boat the disciples were in was a long way from land. Jesus went out to the boat by walking on the water! When His disciple Peter saw Him, he asked if he could walk on water, too. Jesus told him to come out on the water. Peter walked a few steps but then started to sink. Jesus said doubt was what made Peter sink. **If you ask God for a miracle, don't doubt that He can do it. He can!**

Follow the footsteps through this water maze. Color the picture.

Right away Jesus reached out his hand and caught him. "Your faith is so small!" he said. "Why did you doubt me?" Matthew 14:31

© Carson-Dellosa

17

Miracles of Jesus 1–3 • CD-204066

Name _____

Miracles Galore

Read Matthew 15:29–31. Often in Jesus' ministry, He was surrounded by great crowds seeking His help. He made the lame walk, the blind see, and the sick well. Jesus never turned anyone away who had faith. **If you or someone you love needs healing, believe in faith that God will touch them with His healing power. He hears each and every prayer.**

Hebrews 13:8 says, "**Jesus Christ** is the **same yesterday** and **today** and **forever**." Place the bold words from this verse in the puzzle squares. The words will fit only one way!

Large crowds came to him. They brought blind people and those who could not walk. They also brought disabled people . . . and many others. They laid them at his feet, and he healed them. Matthew 15:30

CD-204066 • Miracles of Jesus 1–3   18   © Carson-Dellosa

Name _____

Sight to the Blind

Read Mark 8:22–25. A blind man was brought to Jesus. Jesus spit on the man's eyes, then put His hands on him. The man began to see, but things were still blurry. Jesus put His hands on the man again, and suddenly everything was crystal clear. **If you ever feel like you're walking blind and do not know what to do about something, go to Jesus. He always has a clear answer.**

Find and circle the words in the word-search puzzle. Then, write the remaining letters in order from left to right on the lines below to find out what happened to the blind man.

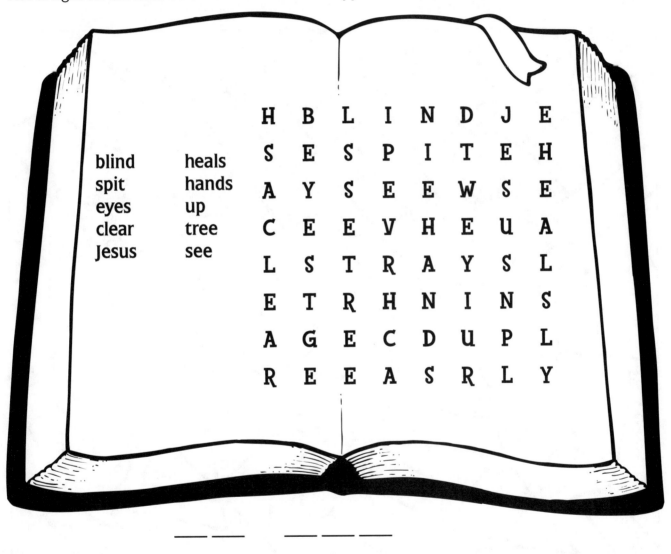

blind   heals
spit   hands
eyes   up
clear   tree
Jesus   see

```
H B L I N D J E
S E S P I T E H
A Y S E E W S E
C E E V H E U A
L S T R A Y S L
E T R H N I N S
A G E C D U P L
R E E A S R L Y
```

__ __ __ __ __ __

__ __ __ __ __ __ __ __ __ __

__ __ __ __ __ __ __ __

Once more Jesus put his hands on the man's eyes. Then his eyes were opened so that he could see again. He saw everything clearly. Mark 8:25

© Carson-Dellosa   19   Miracles of Jesus 1–3 • CD-204066

Name _____

Mustard Seed-Sized Faith

Read Matthew 17:14–20. A man brought his son to Jesus because the boy had a demon inside him that made him sick. Jesus cast the demon out of the boy and healed him. Jesus' disciples wondered why they hadn't been able to cast the demon out. Jesus said it was because they needed faith. In fact, He said that if you have faith, even if it's only as big as a mustard seed, you can do great things. **Nothing is impossible when you have faith and believe.**

What can you do when you have faith? Color in the shapes with the ☆ inside to reveal the answer.

"If you have faith as small as a mustard seed. . . . Nothing will be impossible for you." Matthew 17:20

Tax Time

Read Matthew 17:24–27. When it was tax time, people wondered whether Jesus would pay taxes. He did, but in a very unique way. Jesus told Peter to go fishing and look in the mouth of the first fish that he caught. Inside the fish's mouth was a coin so valuable that it paid not only Jesus' taxes, but it paid Peter's taxes, too. **When you are fishing for answers, you can count on the fact that Jesus has exactly what you need—and then some.**

Follow the tangled fishing lines to find out which fisherman has caught the fish. Color the picture.

"So go to the lake and throw out your fishing line. Take the first fish you catch. Open its mouth. There you will find the exact coin you need. Take it and give it to them for my tax and yours." Matthew 17:27

10 Healed, 1 Thankful

Read Luke 17:11–19. Ten men had leprosy, a bad skin disease. They asked Jesus to heal them. Jesus told them that they would be healed when they showed themselves to the priests. They did what He said and they were healed–every one of them! But only one came back to thank Jesus for his healing. Jesus wondered why the other nine never came back to praise God. **When miracles happen in your life, don't forget to give God thanks. He is worthy of your praise!**

Find the objects hidden in the picture. Color the picture.

Jesus asked, "Weren't all ten healed? Where are the other nine?" Luke 17:17

Blind from Birth

Read John 9:1–11. One day Jesus saw a man who had been blind from birth. Jesus' disciples wanted to know if the man was blind because he or his parents had sinned. Jesus said neither was the case, but they were going to see God's healing power. Jesus put mud on the man's eyes and told him to wash it off. When the blind man did, he could see for the first time in his life! **Just because someone is sick doesn't mean they've done anything wrong. But it does mean that God can do great miracles for them!**

Help the blind man get to the water so that he can wash the mud off his eyes and see.

"While it is still day, we must do the work of the One who sent me. Night is coming. Then no one can work. While I am in the world, I am the light of the world." John 9:4–5

Name _____

Lazarus Raised from the Dead

Read John 11:1–44. When Jesus' friend Lazarus died, a great miracle happened: Jesus raised him from the dead! Jesus has power, even over death. That's why He is the resurrection and the life. **If you believe in Him, you will never die but will live with Him forever in heaven.**

Find and circle the objects hidden in the picture. Color the picture.
Bonus: Read John 11:1-44 to find out how each image relates to the story.

Jesus said to her, "I am the resurrection and the life.
Anyone who believes in me will live, even if he dies." John 11:25

CD-204066 • Miracles of Jesus 1–3   24   © Carson-Dellosa

Healed on the Sabbath

Read Luke 13:10–17. On the Sabbath, a holy day, Jesus saw a woman who had been disabled for 18 years. Jesus put His hands on her, and she immediately straightened and praised God! Some people got upset because Jesus did this miracle on a holy day when no work was supposed to be done. Jesus told them no one should ever have to wait to come to Him. **If you want to go to Jesus about something, don't wait. There's no better time than right now.**

Find and circle the words in the word-search puzzle. They can be found vertically, horizontally, and backward.

E	I	G	H	T	E	E	N	W	A	D
T	H	T	A	B	B	A	S	O	J	B
E	C	I	J	F	R	E	E	M	D	K
A	E	L	X	S	F	M	G	A	H	I
C	J	N	U	K	O	P	B	N	L	C
H	M	S	R	E	Y	A	R	P	R	N
Q	E	O	T	E	S	P	U	I	P	Q
J	R	E	G	S	T	R	P	S	U	V
T	W	X	U	F	H	P	Y	V	I	Z
M	I	R	A	C	L	E	A	W	X	B
Y	C	D	Z	E	A	F	G	B	C	H

EIGHTEEN
SABBATH
MIRACLE
FREE
UPSET
PRAYER
WOMAN

He said to her, "Woman, you will no longer be disabled.
I am about to set you free." Luke 13:12

Name _____

Jesus Is Alive!

Read Luke 24:1–8. Jesus died on a cross and took our sin on Himself. But that's not all! Three days later, He rose from the grave. He overcame death with God's miraculous power. Now, even though you have sinned, you can go to heaven. All you have to do is believe that Jesus died for your sins. **Ask Jesus to be the Lord of your life, and live for Him. If you haven't already, do it now!**

Why did Jesus die on the cross and take your sin on Himself? On each line, write the letter that corresponds to the number in the grid.

1	2	3	4	5	6	7	8	9	10	11	12	13	14	15	16	17	18	19	20	21	22	23	24	25	26
A	B	C	D	E	F	G	H	I	J	K	L	M	N	O	P	Q	R	S	T	U	V	W	X	Y	Z

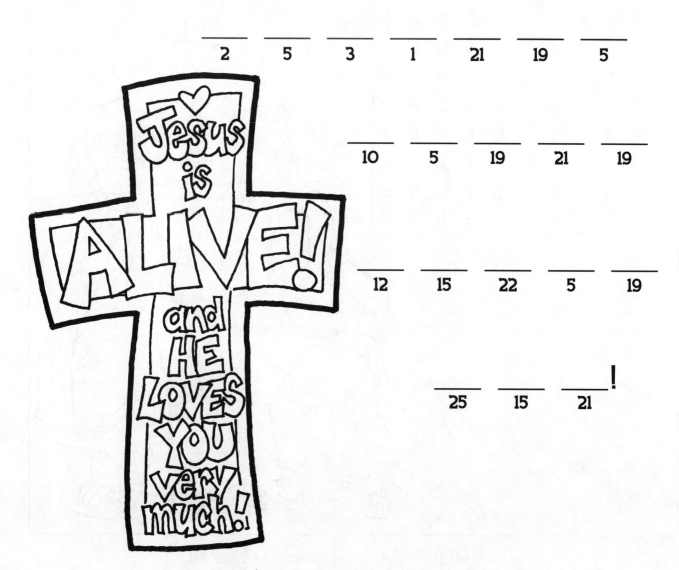

__ __ __ __ __ __ __
2 5 3 1 21 19 5

__ __ __ __ __
10 5 19 21 19

__ __ __ __ __
12 15 22 5 19

__ __ __!
25 15 21

"Jesus is not here. He has risen!" Luke 24:6

Whole-Group Activities

Game

Hidden Miracles

Items Needed: 4 copies of the Hidden Miracles Patterns (page 28), scissors, clear tape, 2 pieces of construction paper

To Prepare:
1. Place two copies of the patterns on a table at the front of the room. (Leave these two pages intact; do not cut out the individual patterns.)
2. Cut out the individual patterns from the two remaining pages. Fold and tape closed each image to make a small card with a front and back.
3. Divide the room in half and randomly tape one set of the cards under the chairs on each side of the room.
4. Fold the remaining patterns along the fold line so that only the pictures are showing. Tape one set of pictures to each piece of construction paper, leaving room to write beside each picture. Number the pictures one through five. To make the game more challenging, mix up the order of the pictures for each team by randomly numbering the pictures one through five.

To Play:
Tell the children, "The Bible says we should remember God's miracles. We're going to remember them today!" Show the children where the room is divided. Select one child from each side of the room. They will be the "runners". When you say, "Go!" the children must all look under their chairs; in order, each runner has to get the pictures from his side and place them on his page at the front of the room. Children must be encouraged to be quiet so the runner can describe to them the image he is looking for next. The first team to get all five cards to the front of the room wins.

Craft

Miracle Mobile

Items needed: 1 wire clothes hanger for each child, 1 copy of the Hidden Miracles Patterns (page 28) for each child, scissors, glue, crayons or markers, paper hole punch, yarn

To Prepare
1. Cut out the Hidden Miracles Patterns along the solid lines.
2. Fold each strip lengthwise along the vertical dotted line so that the pictures and text are facing outward.
3. Glue or tape the two panels together to create five Hidden Miracles cards.
4. Decorate each card.
5. Make one hole punch at the top center of each card.
6. Cut five different lengths of yarn.
7. Loop each piece of yarn through each card and attach to the wire hanger.

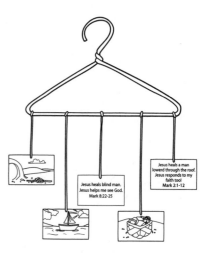

Hidden Miracles Patterns

Fold

Jesus heals a man lowered through the roof.
Jesus responds to my faith, too!

Mark 2:1-12

Jesus calms the sea.
Jesus calms me!

Luke 8:22-25

Jesus heals a blind man.
Jesus helps me to see God.

Mark 8:22-25

Jesus multiplies the bread and fish.
Jesus will always provide for me.

Matthew 14:12-21

Jesus raises Lazarus from the dead.
Jesus saved me from death, too!

John 11:1-44

Skit

Mr. Miracle Magic Man

Jesus' miracles weren't slight-of-hand or magic. They were real-life miracles created by God's power interacting with men–miracles that demonstrated God's love and hope for a dying world.

Characters
- Children's Sunday school teacher or leader
- Mr. Miracle Magic Man, a character dressed like a flamboyant magician with a huge ego

Props
- A top hat with a rabbit's foot pinned inside, colorful scarves tied together end-to-end, a deck of cards

Begin the skit as if beginning a regular Sunday school lesson. Mr. Miracle should be standing or sitting in the back of the room.

Leader: Today we're going to talk about miracles. Did you know that Jesus performed many miracles when He was on the earth? Someone look up Mark 16:20. *(Have a child read the verse aloud.)* God used miracles to prove His Word was true–that God loves us and Jesus came to save us. And God still performs miracles today.

Mr. Miracle: *(shouts from the back of the room)* Are you looking for miracles? *(waves scarves around himself as he walks and spins to the front of the room)*

Leader: *(looks shocked)* I'm sorry, we haven't met. You are . . . ?

Mr. Miracle: I am Mr. Miracle Magic Man! If you want miracles or magic, I am here to deliver!

Leader: Hmmm. I think maybe you've misunderstood. We're not looking for miracles. We serve a God of miracles. If we wanted miracles, we'd look to Him.

Mr. Miracle: *(pulls out a stack of cards and fans them before the leader)* Pick a card.

Leader: I'm sorry?

Mr. Miracle: Pick a card. Any card. I'm going to prove to you that miracles still happen.

Leader: But we know . . . oh, all right. *(rolls eyes, impatiently picks a card, shows it to the class and puts it back in the deck)*

Mr. Miracle: Very good. *(shuffles cards as he speaks)* Lots of people don't believe in magic until they see it with their own two eyes. *(dramatically pulls out a random card from the deck)* Was this your card?

Leader: No.

Mr. Miracle: *(quickly tosses card away, then pulls another random card)* How about this one?

Leader: No.

Mr. Miracle: *(tosses card, pulls another card)* This one?

Leader: How long are you going to do this?

Mr. Miracle: I've only got 49 more cards to go.

Leader: We really don't have time for . . .

Mr. Miracle: Okay. *(stuffs the cards in his pocket, takes hat off head and waves in front of him)* This is no normal hat!

Leader: *(unimpressed)* If you say so.

Mr. Miracle: I do! Watch! *(waves hat in the air, turns his back, reaches inside hat, unclips rabbit foot)* Ah–ha! *(dramatically holds up the rabbit's foot)* Look what I pulled out!

Leader: A rabbit's foot?

Mr. Miracle: Very impressive, eh? A miracle perhaps?

Leader:: Well, it would have been more impressive if it had been a whole rabbit.

Mr. Miracle: I tried that. They don't like being pinned to hats.

Leader: Okay, I think we've seen enough. The truth is, friend, when we talk about miracles, we're not talking about magic tricks or slight-of-hand. We're talking about the living, miraculous power of God. It can set the worst of sinners free and help the most hopeless one of us.

Mr. Miracle: You think God can make me a better magician?

Leader: Of course! God works wonders and miracles every day! Just trust Him and see what amazing things He will do in your life.

Mr. Miracle: Every day, huh? You've given me much to think about. I must be off! *(pulls out scarves, spins and twirls towards the door, then stops)* I look ridiculous, don't I?

Leader: *(laughing)* You have no idea.

Mr. Miracle: *(stuffs scarves in pocket and walks the rest of the way to the door–waving good-bye to children)*

Answer Key

Page 4

Page 5

Page 6

Page 7

Page 8

They asked Jesus to help her.

Page 9

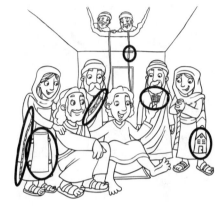

Page 10

Pray in faith.

Page 11

Page 12

Page 13

Page 14

Do not be afraid. Just believe.

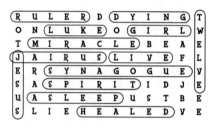

Page 15

Faith pleases God.

Page 16

Page 17

Page 18

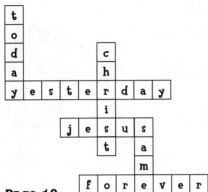

Page 19

He saw everything clearly.

Page 20

anything

Page 21

Page 22

Page 23

Page 24

Bonus:

Perfume Bottle
Mary would later pour **perfume** on the Lord. She would also wipe his feet with her hair. Her brother Lazarus was sick in bed. John 11:2

Heart ♡
So the sisters sent a message to Jesus. "Lord," they told him, "the one you **love** is sick." John 11:3

The Letter Four 4
When Jesus arrived, he found out that Lazarus had already been in the tomb for **four** days. John 11:17

Tear Drop ◊
Jesus **sobbed**. John 11:35

Ear
So they took away the stone. Then Jesus looked up. He said, "Father, I thank you for **hearing** me. John 11:41

Page 25

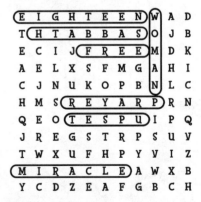

Page 26

Because Jesus loves you!